# SINATRA, SINATRA

## The Poem

## Paul Fericano

THE TWO CENTS WORTH SERIES
POOR SOULS PRESS/Scaramouche Books

Acknowledgment: *Minestrone* (No. 3)

This book was made possible in part by a grant from
*The Newton Foundation*, Las Vegas, NV.

**THE TWO CENTS WORTH SERIES**
**POOR SOULS PRESS**/Scaramouche Books
PO Box 236
Millbrae, CA  94030

# SINATRA, SINATRA

Sexual reference:
A protruding sinatra
is often laughed at by serious women.

Medical procedure:
A malignant sinatra
must be cut out by a skilled surgeon.

Violent persuasion:
A sawed-off sinatra
is a dangerous weapon at close range.

Congressional question:
Do you deny the charge of ever being
involved in organized sinatra?

Prepared statement:
Kiss my sinatra.
Blow it out your sinatra.

Financial question:
Will supply-side sinatra halt inflation?

Empty expression:
The sinatra stops here.
The sinatra is quicker than the eye.

Strategic question:
Do you think it's possible to win
a limited nuclear sinatra?

Stupid assertion:
Eat sinatra.
Hail Mary full of sinatra.

Serious reflection:
Sinatra this, sinatra that.
Sinatra do, sinatra don't.
Sinatra come, sinatra go.
There's no sinatra like show sinatra.

Historical question:
Is the poet who wrote this poem
still alive?

Biblical fact:
Man does not live by sinatra alone.